I0472924

31 Ways to Green Your Business
(And Boost Your Bottom Line.)

Akweli Parker

Copyright © 2011 by Akweli Parker. All rights reserved.

No part of this book may be reproduced in any form or by any
electronic or mechanical means, including information storage and
retrieval systems, without permission in writing from the publisher.
Exceptions are granted to reviewers, who may quote brief excerpts
in their editorial reviews.

Neither the author nor the publisher makes any guarantees
regarding the outcome of the uses to which this material is put, nor
to the suitability of this material to any given purpose.

ISBN-10: 1470160137
ISBN-13: 978-1470160135

Dedicated to all the owners, managers, directors and frontline employees who see sustainability as not just "the right thing to do," but also the smart thing.

CONTENTS

Preface

Is "sustainability" worth pursuing? Can you afford to make it a part of your business? After all, for years, *doing the right thing* by the environment meant necessarily *incurring more costs*.

Those days, however, are fast disappearing. Organizations of all sizes and in all industries are proving that it's possible to profit from a well-thought-out green strategy. In the next few pages you'll find a range of ideas that can work for anyone – from solopreneur to international conglomerate – in running a cleaner and financially *leaner* organization.

Going green isn't just about holding planetary stewardship as a core value, important as that is. Ultimately, it's about capturing the future. The brightest minds in business today herald sustainable practices as the next big driver for gaining strategic competitive advantage. Just as the Internet and computerization did in previous decades, strategies that cut waste and benefit the natural environment will give a major leg up to those companies smart enough to adopt them early.

So review the following suggestions. Figure out which ones make sense for your organization. Start with the "low-hanging fruit" items that you can put in place right away to immediately realize savings. Then let everyone know about your efforts.

There is a positive ripple effect when others observe your achievements and raise their own standards in order to emulate them.

May you meet with great success (and savings) in your pursuit of profitable sustainability!

Akweli Parker

Akweli Parker
Founder, Digital Delta Media

Green Business Tips

Get an energy audit.

Whether you own your own commercial space (or home office) or lease it, any future energy savings you reap will be more meaningful when you have a solid baseline against which to compare. Small businesses and non-profits may even qualify for a free or nominally priced audit, depending on availability of state or local programs.

SAMPLE SMALL BUSINESS SAVINGS

Audit Action	Cost	Annual Savings	Payback (Years)
Upgrade Lighting	$2,681	$683	4.2
Upgrade Programmable Thermostat	$230	$722	0.3
Install High-Efficiency Motors	$8,738	$1,378	6.3
Install LED Exit Signs	$400	$103	3.9
Totals	**$12,229**	**$2,886**	**4.2**

Source: New York State Energy Research and Development Authority

Buy Energy Star-rated equipment.

Energy Star provides helpful rankings for many types of appliances and electronics that consume electricity. Items that appear more inexpensive initially often cost more in the long run because of their inefficiency. So run all the numbers, not just the sticker price, before you buy that next computer!

Participate in e-waste recycling programs.

You can find organizations that will take and recycle your old computers, monitors, printers, cellular phones and other electronics, sometimes for free, sometimes for a small fee. The reputable ones will make sure your unwanted electronics are dismantled responsibly and that salvageable materials are re-used as fully as possible.

Consider "cloud"-based services to save time, money and energy.

The other fancy term used by some techies is "hosted solutions provider." In plain English, that means that someone else maintains and operates the servers and software that run certain parts of your business (for a small fee). You, in turn, save money by not having to pay nearly as much to store servers and keep them cool on your own premises; nor do you have to keep a large IT staff on hand in case equipment or software starts acting buggy. Finally, by putting programs in the cloud, that is, on a wider network such as the

Internet, authorized employees can access them from almost anywhere – extending the reach and effectiveness of your business.

Examine your "supply chain."

Whether you rely on the local Wal-Mart or an assortment of vendors with whom you have official contracts, check their sustainability policies and practices. (Wal-Mart, by the way, is holding its vendors to increasingly stringent standards as part of the company's own ambitious greening effort.)

Consider alternative, renewable energy power suppliers.

In many states, residential, business and industrial customers alike are able to choose from a variety of power suppliers, not just the local utility. Many of these suppliers contract with producers of power that does not come from coal, natural gas or nuclear generation facilities, which all operate with some environmental detriment. Instead, the alternative energy providers source their energy from wind turbines, solar arrays or hydro-electric power. For now, renewable power costs somewhat more up front, but it could provide a great marketing hook to tell customers and prospects that you are "powered 100% by renewable energy." And when hidden, "externalized" costs such as air pollution, waste disposal and habitat destruction are factored in, renewables begin to look much more competitive.

Replace old systems with higher-efficiency ones.

When the old units wear out, get an efficiency upgrade! This applies to more than just electronics: refrigerators, heaters and air conditioners, windows and other "expenses" can be replaced with substitutes that quickly pay for themselves in the form of energy savings. According to Johnson Controls, organizations can save up to 30% on building energy and operating costs through an assortment of conservation and retrofit strategies. For a 250,000 square-foot building, that could be up to a $150,000 savings per year! Further, you may be eligible for tax breaks on the purchase of new, more energy efficient equipment (check with the equipment vendor and your tax preparer).

Buy or lease vehicles that produce low or zero emissions.

The benefit to the environment on this one is something of a no-brainer. Another plus is that vehicles fitting this description are usually fuel misers, meaning a lower cost of operation. And there's yet an additional benefit: a fuel-efficient vehicle sporting your company's logo brands your firm as smart, leading-edge and environmentally sensitive.

Encourage employees to recycle and to be planet-aware.

Reminders can include signs, company-sponsored activities and other awareness builders. Rather than merely pay lip service to environmental stewardship, make it part of the company culture. Some employees may be skeptical at first, but research shows a majority of employees consider a firm's environmental commitment as a factor in their decision to join and stay there.

Join a regional "Green Business" consortium.

There you can learn, leverage and share best practices with other firms. Such green councils are becoming increasingly widespread as companies discover the practical (economic) benefits of being ecologically savvy. If you can't find one that serves your area, consider collaborating with your area's chamber of commerce or fellow business operators to create one!

Permit and encourage telecommuting.

For this to work, you do need responsible, dependable, trustworthy employees. Many studies suggest that the benefits to society and to companies are significant when employees are able to work remotely, even for just a few days a week: it alleviates road congestion, permits employees to achieve a greater sense of life balance, and costs companies less money, as there is a reduced demand on company resources when employees are not in the office. There's even strong evidence that teleworkers are more productive than their office-bound peers!

Skip the individually bottled water.

Provide water cooler service, use tap filters or encourage employees to re-use water containers – rather than purchase one-time-use plastic bottles, which require a lot of energy and resources to make and recycle. Fact: keeping U.S. bottled water drinkers supplied with their plastic-packaged fix of H2O each year consumes nearly 50 million gallons of *oil* – the equivalent of removing 100,000 cars from the road if that oil did not have to be processed and used.

Recycle office cast-offs.

Instead of trashing office furniture that's past its prime, donate it to charity. Alternatively, allow employees to purchase it, and then donate the proceeds to charity.

Use teleconferencing & videoconferencing.

Technology lets you include remote employees in important meetings – keeping everyone on the same page. Options such as Skype, Web conferencing software, and even video call applications on devices like the iPad allow everyone to stay connected and informed, easily and inexpensively, and no matter how far away.

Use online collaboration tools and social intranets to coordinate projects.

You'll need fewer in-person meetings, require less time, and use less paper. You'll also save money, given the large quantities of person hours – units of productivity – that go consumed under-utilized by meetings.

Select the "duplex printing" option on printers and copiers.

For internal, routine print jobs such as meeting agendas and memos, use the reverse side of old (scrap) paper. And as a general habit, avoid printing when an archived electronic copy will do.

Turn computer monitors off at night.

While they do enter a hibernation mode when their attached computer shuts down, they still cause a significant power draw while turned on. This "energy vampire" effect adds up to real money when multiplied by all of the monitors, printers, and other accessories that are often left in a semi-permanent "on" status. According to electric utility Duke Energy, keeping devices plugged in when not in use can account for up to 20 percent of your electricity bill!

Did You Know?

"Thin client" computers with no disk drives and few moving parts are more data-secure than traditional PCs and can be 75% more energy efficient.

Make water conservation "stick."

Place signs or stickers in areas with sink basins to remind employees to run the water efficiently. In bathrooms, install sensor-activated fixtures to automate water conservation.

Fix all drips, leaks, hissing toilets, etc.

Not only do water leaks cost you money now, they could result in even bigger repair bills later by rotting through surrounding areas.

Use energy-efficient lighting.

Fluorescent bulbs use less energy than incandescents. While they cost more to purchase up front, they cost significantly less in the long run because of their energy savings. Most efficient of all are LED lights, which offer the added bonus of converting more of their electric energy into light and less into waste heat, compared to previous room-lighting technologies.

Did You Know?

According to the Environmental Protection Agency, these are a few of the ways you'll save big with each Energy Star-rated light bulb:

- It can save more than $40 in electricity costs over its lifetime

- It uses about 75% less energy than standard incandescent bulbs and lasts at least 6 times longer

- It produces about 75% less heat, so it's safer to operate and can cut energy costs associated with building cooling

Publicize your efforts to both internal and external audiences.

A number of research studies suggest that "green" businesses tend to perform better financially and have more engaged workforces, resulting in a "virtuous cycle" between employee satisfaction and business results.

Encourage non-automotive means for employees to get to work.

Distribute pedometers, install bike racks and even offer incentives for staff to get active in their commutes. Provide access to lockers and showers, if feasible (for instance, if you already have an on-site fitness center). Provide a discount to users of mass transit. Bonus: physically active employees cost less across the board – lower healthcare costs plus lower absentee rates. According to articles published in the *American Journal of Health Promotion*, corporate employee wellness programs studied by researchers yielded returns on investment between 3-to-1 and 5-to-1!

Need training or certifications?

Promote distance learning, in the form of online classes, as part of your organization's training curriculum. Online learning slashes expenses for travel and lodging, and allows learning to take place on a schedule more convenient for employees – and your business.

Apply Lean Six Sigma ...

... *and* other principles of high quality, low waste, to your operations. Higher quality results in less rework, fewer returns from customers, and ultimately, lower costs for the business. Waste is merely a function of efficiency. Waste can be worker effort that does not contribute to the finished product or it can be non-utilization of some of the materials used to make a product. In both cases, efforts to be more efficient have a double bottom line – they save money for the business and they're less taxing on the environment.

Use GPS receivers to prevent getting lost and wasting fuel, and to save time.

If you've ever made a bad impression because you got lost on the way to a business appointment, you know how important this one can be. If you have a fleet of vehicles that routinely travel to unfamiliar places, GPS is a no-brainer. Systems can be as simple as a $100 unit purchased at an electronics retailer or as elaborate as fleet tracking services that let you know where any vehicle in your fleet is at any moment.

Pull down the shades on extremely hot days.

(And raise them on very cold ones). Such "passive" cooling and heating goes a long way toward taking the load off your building's HVAC system. And that takes a load off of your expenses, whether you're a building owner or a tenant who has to foot part of the utility bill.

Install windows with high-efficiency glazing.

Modern windows come available with coatings and gas-filled inner spaces that make them 40% more energy efficient than traditional windows.

Avoid over-cooling or over-heating buildings.

You'll probably get lots of feedback as to what's "too hot" or "too cold," but the general consensus is that around 72 degrees Fahrenheit (22 degrees centigrade) is just right.

Turn off the lights in rooms when they're not in use.

That includes personal offices! You can make compliance less of a hassle by putting in sensors that shut off the lights automatically when a room is unoccupied.

Go paperless – both sending and receiving.

Many companies have taken to actually charging customers extra to receive paper statements and other communications. You can set up secure forms on your Web site for customers to submit documentation and otherwise interact with your organization. Once again, doing a favor for the environment – using less paper – results in savings for your bottom line.

Use car-sharing versus buying or leasing.

Meetings at branch locations, sales calls and off-site work all require travel by car. But cars sit idle close to 90 percent of the time! In business, an under-utilized asset quickly becomes a liability when it fails to pay for itself. But if you work in or near a large city, a *car-sharing service* gives you access to an assortment of autos, when you need them, and at far less than the cost of traditional renting, leasing or outright ownership. It also takes cars off the road, thereby reducing traffic congestion, pollution and danger to pedestrians and bicyclists!

Closing Thoughts

Now that you're aware of the many ways you can green your organization, you may have quite a few questions on just how to go about it. For example, which of these tactics are most appropriate for your organization? Which will save the most money for your particular situation? How do you establish a strategic framework for implementing them? And, if you do have employees, how do you best engage them to understand and embrace your values concerning sustainability?

The good news is that you no longer have to address these issues in a vacuum. Business people, academics, journalists and others have devoted considerable study and analysis to enhancing the Triple Bottom Line – that is, the financial, environmental and social benefits of running an organization conscientiously.

For larger organizations, consultancies will come in and help install an entire global sustainability strategy that touches every business unit. For smaller organizations, effective change can begin with relatively simple tracking tools – for instance, Excel spreadsheets that are widely available online.

Resources such as this guidebook and the Web sites listed at its conclusion provide solid examples you can use now, as well as further areas to explore. As an example, the Internal Revenue Service offers guidance on deductions you can take for energy-efficient commercial buildings.

Communicating the Greening of Your Organization. Many people dispute that there even *is* a need to curb carbon emissions and conserve natural resources. In a workplace context, management has the responsibility of explaining why sustainability is a core value of the organization. It's important to explain that the long-term health of the organization hinges on adopting sustainable practices.

As developing nations continue their economic advances, once-cheap and abundant resources will become scarcer and more expensive. That means existing companies and other organizations must innovate if they wish to survive. For employees, their livelihoods and the collective health of their communities depend on their increased efficiency. And, it just so turns out, the natural environment wins in the bargain, too.

ADDITIONAL RESOURCES

Database of State Incentives for Renewables & Efficiency
www.dsireusa.org/

Green Building Initiative
www.thegbi.org/

Internal Revenue Service
irs.gov/

Department of Energy - Green Power Network
eere.energy.gov/greenpower/

Environmental Protection Agency - Energy Star
www.energystar.gov/

EPA - Green Power Partnership
www.epa.gov/greenpower/

U.S. Green Building Council
www.usgbc.org/

Share the Knowledge!

You can order customized reprints of this booklet, featuring your organization's logo and an introductory message from your chief executive or other leader. It's perfect as a handout to share throughout your entire organization, to distribute at trade shows, or to serve as a memorable and useful resource to clients and prospects.

For custom ordering, simply send an email with your name, organization and contact information to:

info@digitaldeltamedia.com

or call toll free: 855-433-6334

Additional electronic or paper copies of this booklet may be ordered directly (without customizing) by visiting **amazon.com**

For more tips, articles, and videos, visit

digitaldeltamedia.com/ green

NOTES

_____

_____

_____

_____

_____

_____

_____

_____

_____

www.ingramcontent.com/pod-product-compliance
Lightning Source LLC
Chambersburg PA
CBHW071552170526
45166CB00004B/1644